Finding Out About
STREAMS

John Bentley and
Bill Charlton

Batsford Academic and Educational   *London*

~~~ Contents ~~~

Typeset by Tek-Art Ltd, Kent
and printed in Great Britain
by R.J. Acford
Chichester, Sussex
for the publishers
Batsford Academic and Educational,
an imprint of B. T. Batsford Ltd,
4 Fitzhardinge Street
London W1H 0AH

ISBN 0 7134 4425 8

ACKNOWLEDGMENTS

The Authors and Publishers would like to thank the following for their kind permission to reproduce illustrations: G.L.C. London Fire Brigade Photographic Service, page 8; Kent County Council, pages 44 and 45; The Ordnance Survey, pages 38 and 39 (below), from OS Sheet TQ 3968, 1898 and 1936. All other photographs and diagrams in the book and on the cover are copyright of the Authors. Special thanks are expressed to John Marshall for the photographic prints.

Cover picture
The colour picture on the front cover shows a shallow stretch of the River Darenth close to its source near Westerham, Kent.

~~Introduction~~

Ask anyone to draw a sketch of a typical British landscape and the chances are that you will find a stream in it somewhere. This isn't surprising because streams are very common features in Britain. Most parts of the country get plenty of rainfall – and that means plenty of water to flow away into the sea. Furthermore, streams are an important part of the natural environment. The shapes of our hillsides and valleys are partly the result of the work of the streams as they wear away the land. Without the streams, our scenery would look very different.

Perhaps more important are the many ways in which streams, right from earliest times, have influenced people's everyday lives. Mostly they have brought benefits and advantages. In the past, local streams provided our ancestors with essential resources like water and fish. Streams turned water wheels, and the line of a stream was often used to mark the boundary of village lands. Nowadays, the importance of streams is more often seen in terms of leisure activities like angling – or just paddling and picnics. On the other hand, our streams have sometimes shown the unkind side of their nature. In times of flood they have destroyed crops, swept away bridges and even caused loss of life.

Generally speaking, when we talk about a stream we mean something smaller than a river. However, the action of flowing water is just the same in a stream as in a river. Only the scale is different. This means that if you find out about streams you are also finding out about rivers. It is much easier, of course, to study streams than rivers, and that is why the work in this book is mainly about streams. However, every now and then you will be asked something about rivers too – to remind you that rivers are just the same as streams, only bigger.

This kind of study – in which you find out about the environment, and the way people use it – is part of the subject of geography. The work involves a number of different activities, including the study of maps and books. The most important method of finding out, however, will be to make visits to local streams to see things for yourself, collect materials, take measurements and make maps and drawings. This kind of work, called field-work, is an important way of studying geography.

Usually the only equipment you will need for your field-work is a clip-board, paper, notebook and pencil, but sometimes you will also need a tape measure and a metre rule or some polythene bags for specimens. Most of the work you are asked to do could be done on your own, but you will find the field-work more enjoyable with a friend, or in a group.

In order to carry out some of the work you are asked to do you will have to find a stream to study. When you are carrying out this search, remember that the smaller streams are easier to study. Remember also that even small streams can sometimes be dangerous because the depth of the water can be treacherous and currents can sometimes sweep you off your feet. You have to choose your spot carefully and check the safety with a grown-up.

If you live near an upland or mountainous area, you will probably have no difficulty in finding a suitable stream. In lowland areas you may not be so lucky, because many streams are in private property and you may need to ask permission before you can get to them. Suitable streams can be difficult to locate in towns, too, though you will often find them as attractive features in parks.

One of the things you will find out about streams is that their condition can change very considerably depending on the weather. Furthermore, the vegetation on the banks varies according to the season of the year. So try to make a series of visits, and time them according to variations in the weather.

Useful Sources

Your most important source of information is the stream itself. Much of the finding out suggested in this book starts from your own field-work and investigates along, around and, very often, in your local stream. Each stream is unique and presents the excitement of real discovery. So, with your notepad and pencil, wellingtons and equipment for collecting samples or measuring, off you go and explore. When you have made your observations the following methods and resources will help you to continue your discoveries.

1. MAPS

You need to make many of your own maps and sketches when following the ideas in this book. At first, keep your maps very simple and concentrate on small stretches of streams, no more than 5 or 10 metres in length. With practice, your map skills will soon develop. It is a good idea to make a neat copy of your drawing as soon as you are home or back in the classroom. It can be surprising how quickly you forget the detail of your own notes or sketches.

(i) *Ordnance Survey Maps* When you need an accurate survey of a small area for your studies the most useful maps are the large-scale plans published by the Ordnance Survey. The largest useful scales are:

1 : 2,500 (40 cm to 1 km or approx. 25" to 1 mile)
1 : 10,000 (10 cm to 1 km or approx. 10" to 1 mile)

These plans or maps are the best for practical field-work because they show such detail as the width of the stream, details of the stream banks and the location of distinctive features like individual trees or fences. You can also use these maps to make enlargements of a small section of stream for your field-work.

On the following map scales of the Ordnance Survey less detail is shown but the areas covered are much larger:

1 : 25,000 (4 cm to 1 km or approx. 2½" to 1 mile)
1 : 50,000 (2 cm to 1 km or approx. 1" to 1 mile)

These maps are best for the study of patterns in the landscape; particularly for the study of stream networks and the contour patterns of valleys. Also these map scales illustrate very clearly the ways in which streams and rivers affect human activity (e.g. as barriers and bridging points) or provide resources, that is "useful things" such as water power sites, recreation areas, boundary lines and valley routeways.

Information about the Ordnance Survey maps is available from the Director General, The Ordnance Survey, Romsey Road, Maybush, Southampton SO9 4DH.

(ii) *Atlases* These books provide maps of the smallest scales and the largest areas. They are no use for the detailed study of local streams but they are important in finding out about the very biggest streams, the rivers of the world. They emphasize too the significance of flowing water which shapes the land and influences where people live. See if you can find a major inland city which is not on a river. Atlas maps also show clearly the network patterns made by rivers and you can pick out the shape and extent of individual drainage basins within a country or continent (see page 26).

2. GOVERNMENT DEPARTMENTS AND NATIONAL ASSOCIATIONS

There are many national bodies interested in and responsible for the management of water resources whether in terms of water supply, flood control or amenity and recreation. Here are just a few of them which can provide some starting points for you.

(i) *Department of the Environment* 2 Marsham Street, London SW1P 3EB. There are also regional offices in Birmingham, Leeds, Manchester, Newcastle, Bristol, Nottingham, N. Ireland. These can all provide information relating to the presence and use of water, particularly in the context of planning.

(ii) *Water Authorities Association,* 1 Queen Anne's Gate, London SW1H 9BT. There are also 10 regional water authorities in England and Wales and 9 Scottish regional councils which are responsible for the recording and management of all water resources within their areas. Their responsibilities were outlined and organized by the Water Act of 1983. The addresses for each of these authorities can be obtained from your local library or they can be found on your parents' water rate.

(iii) *Countryside Commission,* John Dower House, Crescent Place, Cheltenham, Glos. GL50 3RA.

(iv) *Nature Conservancy Council (N.C.C.),* 19-20 Belgrave Square, London SW1X 8BY. These last two organizations are representative of a wide range of bodies interested in the environment at large but which can provide particular references and information about streams in the landscape. Your local library can help you with more.

3. COUNTY COUNCILS AND DISTRICT COUNCIL
    OFFICES

There are various departments within local authorities which can provide useful information on the use and control of water in the environment. The county councils, for example, are responsible for the planning of a region's resources and this will include plans similar to the Stour Valley Countryside Plan of the Kent County Council (see page 44). In the local council offices the county structure plans can be consulted and the local planning department can inform you about schemes and policies associated with the local streams and rivers. Local councils are also responsible,

Follow the Country Code

Guard against all risk of fire
Fasten all gates
Keep dogs under proper control
Keep to the paths across farm land
Avoid damaging fences, hedges and walls
Leave no litter
Safeguard water supplies
Protect wild life, wild plants and trees
Go carefully on country roads
Respect the life of the countryside

The waymark sign is used in plaque or stencil form by the Countryside Commission on long-distance routes.

Countryside Commission, John Dower House, Crescent Place, Cheltenham, Glos GL50 3RA. Tel: Cheltenham (0242) 21381

generally through the engineers' department, for the control and maintenance of sewerage and storm water schemes. Here again you can ask them for information about the provision of these important services.

4. LIBRARIES

Libraries have a wide range of useful materials and lists of organizations and you should ask a librarian for guidance. Local libraries will be able to help you with the names and addresses of national and local bodies concerned with the use of streams: e.g. angling clubs, water sports, natural history and conservation societies. Local libraries will also have large-scale maps of different dates which will enable you to trace the streams past and present of your local area. From the maps the location of old water mills can often be discovered and in most areas now it is possible to visit an old water mill which has been restored to working order. Again, ask your librarian for information about local mills or museums of industrial archaeology.

Finally, in all your finding out about streams, remember these three things:

1. Water can be dangerous so always let adults know when and where you are going and observe all safety regulations.

2. Always seek advice and permission from local landowners or park keepers. They can be very helpful in telling you about the history and character of local streams.

3. Observe the country code.

Streams in the Water Cycle

The sight and sound of rainfall are common enough – at least to us in Britain, where we can expect rain on about 100 days every year. Can you remember the number of rainy days you have had during the last two weeks? The amount of rain that falls varies from place to place, more if you live in the west of the country and less if you live in the east. If you have a good atlas you can find out how much variation there is. Find out which are the wettest areas and which are the driest, and how much rainfall they get.

Rainfall varies not only in amount, but also in the intensity with which it falls. Rain drops vary in size from the fine, spray-like droplets of drizzle to the large, "wet" drops of thunder showers. And the bigger they are the faster and harder they fall. The downpour from a thunderstorm can release, in a few minutes, more water than a whole day of drizzle – and it produces very different results on the ground. The next time it rains, watch what happens to the water as it falls on different kinds of surfaces. Where does the water go? Does it soak into the ground or collect in pools or flow away? Keep a regular watch on a hard area (like a playground) and draw a plan to show those parts where you find pools, and which way

◁ *The rainwater which flows into drains is part of the water cycle. What are the other visible signs of the water cycle?*

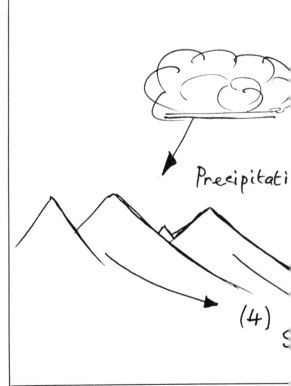

Precipitati

(4)

water flows away into the drains.

Falling rain and the flow of water on the surface of the land are two of the stages in what is known as the "water cycle" – or "hydrological cycle", to give its scientific name. Water evaporates into the atmosphere as a gas (water vapour), falls as rain, flows into the sea, or into lakes, and evaporates again. Why do you think this is called a "cycle"?

This book is about streams, but in order to understand them properly we need to see how they link up with the other water in our environment. The water we see moving through our environment – as clouds, as rain or snow, as streams, or even as steam rising from a wet pavement or fence – is all part of the water cycle. Even the ice in mountain glaciers, or in the ice-caps of the polar regions, is part of the same cycle, though in these cases the water may be "stored" for perhaps hundreds of years before it melts and starts to move through the cycle again.

Here in Britain the water cycle influences our everyday lives and activities in a great many ways – think of the effect of rainfall, for example, on the clothes we wear, on driving conditions, or on sporting activities. It particularly influences the way we build. Look carefully at the houses and streets of your own neighbourhood and make a list of all the methods and materials that are used to control and direct the flow of rainwater so that it doesn't get into places where it could do damage. Can you think of any unfortunate results which can occur when our attempts to control the flow of water are not successful?

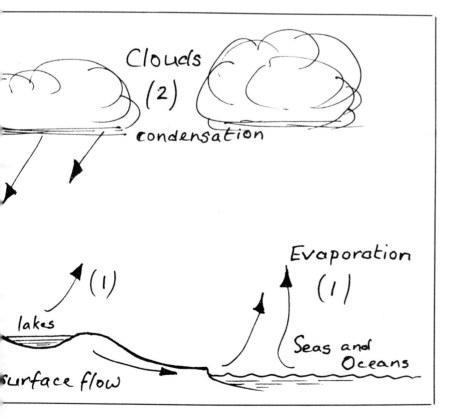

Clouds
(2)
condensation

Evaporation
(1)

lakes

(1)

surface flow

Seas and
Oceans

The hydrological cycle. All the water circulating around the world is part of an endless process of change. The four repeating stages in this continuous cycle are:
1) Evaporation (the change into water vapour, an invisible gas)
2) Condensation (the change from water vapour to ice crystals or water droplets)
3) Precipitation (the fall of rain, snow, hail, etc, and the deposition of dew and frost)
4) Surface flow (water as liquid in streams, rivers, lakes, oceans, etc).

Flowing Water

~~~~~~~~~~~~

It requires the strength of two firemen to hold this hose steady. The great force of water from high pressure hoses is also used in some mining operations. It is known as hydraulic mining. China clay from Cornwall is mined in this way. Can you think of other uses of strong jets of water?

To say that the water in a stream flows downhill may seem so obvious as to be hardly worth mentioning, but behind this simple fact lies the secret of the enormous power of streams and rivers to alter the shape of the land. The power of a stream comes from the energy which is present in the movement of the water as it flows, by the force of gravity, from its source in hills or mountains to its mouth in a lake or in the sea.

All moving objects contain energy, and the energy allows them to do work – like the energy in a moving hammer which bangs in a nail. If you stand in a stream you can feel the energy in the water as it pushes against your legs, and if the stream is big enough there might even be enough energy to knock you over.

Right from the beginning of history people have used the energy in flowing water to do useful work, such as turning water wheels. Even nowadays we put this energy to good use – in a hydro-electric power station, for example, where the energy in flowing water is converted into electricity. In the days before the industrial revolution moving water was the most powerful source of energy used by man, and it is still important in many parts of today's world.

Moving water can be very powerful indeed, and sometimes we can actually see this power. Why do you think two firemen are needed to hold a hose steady when they are fighting a fire? You can find out about this for yourself by doing a simple experiment with a garden hosepipe. Turn on the tap so that the water comes out fairly gently and then press your thumb over the end of the hosepipe to concentrate the flow into a jet. All the energy of the flow of water is now concentrated in the jet and if you direct it against lumps of soil or pebbles you will be able to move them quite easily. Imagine how much more energy there will be in even a small stream.

The amount of energy in a stream depends partly on the quantity of water and partly on the difference in height between the source and the mouth. More water and a greater fall will produce more energy; but however much energy there is, it is all used up as the stream gradually makes its way down to its mouth.

Electricity is generated when the water held behind this dam flows down through turbines in the power station. This is called hydro-electric power.

The work which results from the using up of this energy is what creates the valley and its features. (See pages 24-25.) Where streams flow continuously (as most of our streams do in Britain), this work never ceases and the shapes of their valleys are constantly changing.

The Stream Channel

The "channel" is the name given to the groove in the surface of the land which contains the flowing water of the stream, concentrating and directing its energy. After heavy rain a channel may be full right up to the brim. At other times, say during a dry spell during the summer, the stream is no more than a trickle and the channel appears almost empty. It is by studying the channel of a stream that you can begin to find out about the work of flowing water.

The best way to study a stream channel is to go and look at an actual example – in other words, carry out a "field-study". In order to do the kind of work described in this chapter you need to find a fairly small stream, no more than a few metres wide and shallow enough for wellington boots. When you have found a suitable stream, you have to decide on a section on which to concentrate – ideally about 10 metres long. You are going to find out how the shape of the channel varies from place to place along the stream, and you do this in two ways: by measuring *across* the channel and then *along* the channel. You will need some equipment – a tape measure, a measuring rod

(e.g. a metre rule) and a notebook and pencil.

First, see if you can measure the variations in the shape of the channel *across* the stream. Choose a spot along your stretch of stream and measure the distance from one bank to the other. This is called the "channel width". You should measure directly across the stream from the top of each bank, and you may have problems because it is not always easy to say exactly where the top of the bank is. You have to decide. Next, you measure the width of the water itself. Then, stretching your tape measure across the stream and dipping your measuring rod into the water, you make a note of the depth of the water at different points across the channel. (Remember that the depth of the water will vary from day to day – or even from hour to hour – as the water level rises or falls.) All these details are shown in the diagram. This kind of diagram is a "cross section".

Channel depth can be measured as the distance between bank top level and the stream bed. A length of string stretched across the channel gives you a line from which to measure down to the channel bed.

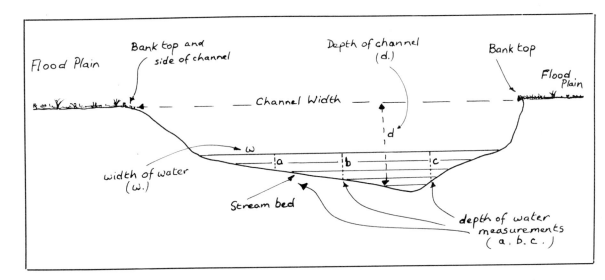

Canals are man-made channels and their banks are straight and regular, unlike the irregular banks of natural streams. Why does the width of the canal vary?

Now you can turn your attention to the variations *along* the stream channel. Stand where you can see your study section clearly and sketch as carefully as you can the outline of the banks and the water surface. If you walk slowly along your section, you may notice that patches of deeper, stiller water (called "pools") alternate with patches of shallower, swiftly-flowing turbulent water (called "riffles"). Mark the position of these pools and riffles on your sketch map.

The information you have collected from this field-work will help you to write a short description of your stream channel, mentioning variations both across and along the stream. Illustrate your account with a neat copy of the sketch map you drew. If you can get help from your teacher, or anyone who understands scale drawings, you could also use your information to draw some cross sections.

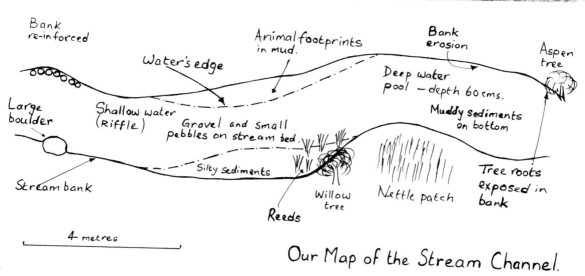

Bank re-inforced

Animal footprints in mud.

Bank erosion

Aspen tree

Water's edge

Deep water pool – depth 60 cms.

Large boulder

Shallow water (Riffle)

Gravel and small pebbles on stream bed.

Muddy sediments on bottom

Silty sediments

Stream bank

Willow tree

Nettle patch

Tree roots exposed in bank

Reeds

4 metres

Our Map of the Stream Channel.

Banks and Beds ~~~~~~~~

It is helpful to think of the channel of a stream in two parts – the stream bed on the bottom and the banks at each side. Together they concentrate and direct the flow of water down the valley. The change from bed to bank is not always easy to see because the slope from one to the other can be very gentle.

The first evidence of stream work you can examine is the nature of the material which makes up the bed and the banks. Find a good place beside a stream where you can easily and safely study the channel and see how many different kinds of material you can find. If you take a clip-board and a pencil you can record your observations on the spot; then you

won't forget anything. Take some plastic bags, too, so that you can collect some samples, and a tape measure.

In some parts of the stream bed the water may flow over solid rock; elsewhere there may be boulders and large rocks with pebbles in between, or fine silt. There will probably be a similar variety in the material of the banks, though it may not be so obvious if the banks are covered by growing vegetation.

Collect some samples of the different materials and put them in your plastic bags, remembering to number them and make a note of where you found each sample. Where rocks and boulders are too big to carry away, use your tape measure to find out how big they

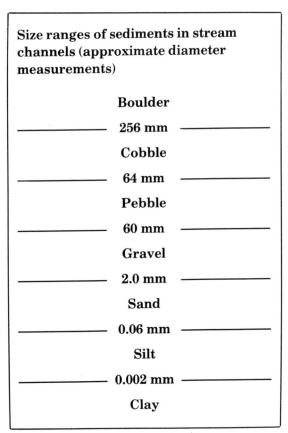

Size ranges of sediments in stream channels (approximate diameter measurements)

Boulder
——————— 256 mm ———————
Cobble
——————— 64 mm ———————
Pebble
——————— 60 mm ———————
Gravel
——————— 2.0 mm ———————
Sand
——————— 0.06 mm ———————
Silt
——————— 0.002 mm ———————
Clay

How much variety can you see in the materials which ▷ form this river bank?

are and note this down, too. When you have noted everything you can find, move a few yards upstream or downstream and have another search. Afterwards, at home or at school, when your samples have dried, you can look at each one separately and make an analysis of the contents.

The table on page 12 shows how scientists grade the sediments in a stream according to their size. Use a magnifying glass to study your samples against a ruler marked in centimetres and millimetres. See if you can identify any of the grades of sediment described in the table. You will probably find that the finest particles are too small to be separately identified.

The information you have collected from your samples and the notes you made beside the stream should give you enough to write a short account called "Materials in the Stream Channel" (and don't forget to mention those you were not able to bring away!)

There are also some questions you can think about. Why are there so many different kinds of material in a stream channel? Where have they all come from? Why are some of them concentrated in certain places? Is there any difference between the materials in the bed and those in the banks? You may be able to answer some of these questions straightaway. For others, you will have to read on through the book to find the explanations.

Currents

~~~~~~~~~~~~~~~

From the moment that water bubbles from a spring or seeps from the earth and begins its journey downstream, the speed of the flowing water varies considerably. At different points along the stream and at different times throughout the year you can see these variations quite clearly. Where the movement of water has a definite direction and velocity (speed) we refer to it as the "current". Even within a small section of a stream you are likely to find variations in current. You can pick out the eddies and swirls of the current if you look down from a bridge. Look particularly at the places where the flow of water meets the supports of the bridge. You will find parts of the stream where the current appears to flow faster and others where there seems to be no flow at all. Where there are boulders or other

The pebbles, branches and other materials in this stream interrupt the flow of the water and direct the current from side to side forming whirlpools and eddies.

obstructions to the flow of the water you can probably identify several quite separate threads, or lines, of current. In the photograph above the turbulent water shows where the current is strong while other parts show little sign of any current. These variations in the speed and direction of currents are very important because they control the way the stream is using its energy (see pages 8-9). In this way, the changes in velocity help to shape the bed and banks of the stream channel.

Choose a small section of a stream, about 5 metres long, where you can stand safely on the

edge of the channel and see across and down the stream. Draw a neat sketch plan of your section of stream. Look directly across the channel and see if you can spot any variations in the current. Does the water seem to be flowing at the same speed right across its width? Mark a line of arrows on your plan where the current appears to be quicker.

When you have made your observations looking across the channel, turn and see if you can find any current changes in a downstream direction. Does the current move from one side to the other or does it keep to the centre of the channel? Put a small twig or piece of wood in the stream close to where you are and mark a dotted line on your sketch map to show the course it takes as it floats downstream. If you put several sticks in at different points across the channel, do they all move downstream at the same speed? Have some races with your sticks placed at different points across the

This specially designed weir with its scientific apparatus is a way of measuring the flow of a stream very accurately. It is used by hydrologists.

stream and see which position wins most often. If you have a watch which shows seconds, measure the shortest time it takes for a stick to travel the 5 metres down the course of the stream. You should make a record of all your observations, describing what happens to each of the sticks. Are there any places where the current is much slower? What kind of obstructions alter the direction and speed of the current? When you have completed all your observations and made all your notes, you can draw a large, neat copy of your map and mark on it all the information you have. Add a key to explain any symbols you have used, and give it a title – "Currents in a Stream".

Erosion

Have you noticed that the water in a stream is sometimes muddy? If you look closely you can actually see particles of mud and sand being swept along. This material has been worn away from the stream channel and is carried away by the flowing water. The wearing-away process is called "erosion" and the material which has been eroded from the land and is being carried along in the water is called the "load" of the stream. Erosion takes place all the time, but we notice it most after there has been heavy rainfall, i.e. when there is lots of fast-flowing water in the streams.

You found out about the energy in flowing water on pages 8-9, and it is this energy which gives a stream the power to erode the land. The force of the moving water is enough on its own to move loose material along in the current. A gently flowing stream can move only small particles, but a raging torrent can shift large boulders. Once this material is moving along as part of the load of the stream, it helps the process of erosion by chipping away other pieces of rock or soil as it is thrown by the current against the bed and the banks.

On most occasions when you look at a stream the water level will be quite low. When there is very little water flowing it is hard to believe that erosion is really going on. You have to remember that most of the erosion happens after wet weather when the stream is surging down the valley, right up to the top of its banks. The eroding power of a stream becomes much greater as the quantity and

Soil has been washed away from the concrete foundations of this bridge.

speed of the water increase. Erosion is greatest when the stream is at the "bank-full" state.

The evidence of erosion is present almost everywhere along the course of a stream. You can look for this evidence and try to work out why erosion is taking place more rapidly in some places than in others. Collect a sample of water from a place where the current is fast, and another from where it is slow. Let the water settle for a few hours and then compare the amounts of sediment you find and the size of the particles. Which one do you think will have more?

Those parts of the banks which are being eroded most quickly are often bare of growing vegetation. Can you think how vegetation can protect the banks from erosion? Why should erosion be more severe on the outside of

All these pebbles and boulders have been smoothed and rounded by erosion. Where else can you find sediments shaped by water in this way?

bends than on the inside? The erosion of the banks often causes problems, as in the photograph on the left, and you may find that engineers or farmers have tried to protect the banks with a concrete wall or wooden piles.

If your stream has pebbles or boulders in its channel, notice how they have been made smooth by the action of erosion. The gradual wearing-away of the pebbles and boulders and all the other materials in the stream by knocking against each other is called "attrition". Have you ever used a stone-polisher? It is exactly the same process, but in the case of the stream it goes on for ever.

Deposition

All the eroded material we found out about on pages 16-17 is eventually transported by the stream into the sea (or a lake). The greater the speed of flowing water, the greater the amount of materials like mud and pebbles that can be moved downstream. The fast-flowing floodwaters of a stream always look muddy because of the load of sediments that is being carried along "in suspension". As long as the water continues to flow at the same speed, the same load of sediment can be transported; but once the velocity (and therefore the energy) of the stream begins to decrease, some of the material has to be deposited on the bed and sides of the channel. The largest and heaviest pebbles are the first to be deposited and, if the speed of the current continues to fall, the size and weight of the material that can be carried are progressively reduced. Eventually, when the current has slowed right down, only the

This delta has been formed where a tiny stream flows into the still water of Alcock Tarn in the Lake District.

finest particles of mud and silt can be carried along.

You can see, then, that the process of deposition depends very much on the speed of the water. If the speed of the current falls, part of the stream's load is deposited. However, if the velocity increases, sediment is picked up from the stream bed and banks and transported further downstream. As we have seen (pages 14-15), there are many variations in the current within a stream, and this means that pebbles and sediment in the stream channel can have a very irregular journey, stopping and starting on their way downstream. At what time of the year are pebbles likely to make most progress downstream?

Anything which causes the velocity of flowing water to decrease produces some form of deposition. How many things can you think of that might cause this to happen? Have a look again at what you did on pages 12-13 and see if you can find reasons for the kinds of deposition you found.

Deposition produces some distinctive features along the course of the channel and you can see one of them in the photograph. This delta has formed where the speed of the current has been abruptly slowed as the stream enters the still waters of the lake. The decrease in the current has caused the stream's sediment load to be deposited and over the years it has gradually built up to produce the delta. What do you think will happen to the lake as the delta continues to grow? What problems could the process of deposition cause in reservoirs that store and supply water for hydro-electric power stations? Find out from an encyclopaedia why these features of river deposition are called "deltas". Some of the world's largest rivers have formed deltas at their mouths. There is a list of them below. Find these rivers in your atlas and draw a set of maps to show the location and shape of their deltas. You should indicate the name of the country through which the river flows, the sea which it enters, and any large cities nearby. Remember to add a scale to your maps.

These large rivers all have deltas:

Amazon
Ganges
Mekong
Mississippi
Niger
Nile
Orinoco
Rhine
Volga

Meanders

~~~~~~~~~~~~~~~~~~~~   ~~~~~~~~~~~~

In your work on streams, have you seen any straight channels? Water rarely flows in a straight line and generally a stream has many bends and loops in its course. If you do find an absolutely straight stream channel it is virtually certain to be the work of man, improving the drainage of the land or seeking to control the flow of water (see pages 36-37). Where a stream flows through a flood plain, you sometimes find a whole series of loops called "meanders". In the photograph you can see a typical example. The word "meander" actually comes from the name of a river in Turkey which has a great many of these sinuous bends.

A meandering section of a stream is a good place to find out more about the work of streams, because meanders have distinctive shapes and the flow of water follows a regular course. You will find that several of the activities dealt with separately in earlier sections of this book are brought together in the study of meanders.

Before you start your investigations, you will need to make a sketch map of a meandering stretch of stream. Choose a section about 20 to 30 metres long, which has about two or three definite loops as shown in the photograph. Use the method described on pages 14-15 to explore the variation in the current across and along the channel. You will notice considerable differences in the speed of the flowing water and you should note on your map where the water is slow-moving (perhaps even still) and where there is a line of definite current. Mark this line along the channel on your map, observing carefully how the thread of fast-flowing water moves from side to side along the channel. Can you locate where the cross-over points occur?

The meandering stream is nearly "bank-full". Notice how the erosion is cutting away the banks on the outside of the bends where the current is strongest. Where would you expect to find deposition after the water level has fallen?

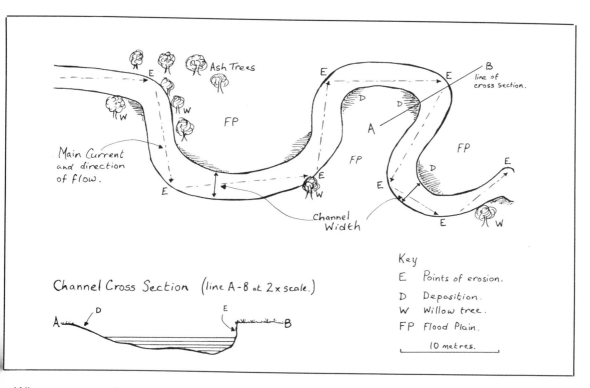

Inside the figure:

Ash Trees

E

W

FP

Main Current
and direction
of flow.

E

E

D

D

A

FP

FP

E

W

Channel
Width

E

E

B
line of
cross section.

D

E

E

W

Channel Cross Section   (line A–B at 2x scale.)

A   D

E

B

Key
E   Points of erosion.
D   Deposition.
W   Willow tree.
FP   Flood Plain.

10 metres.

A meandering stream.

When you have completed your observations on variations in current, turn your attention to the features of erosion and deposition along the banks (see pages 16-19) and locate them on your map. Use different symbols or letters to distinguish between erosion and deposition. Give each of these features a number and, for each one, note how you can tell whether it is a feature of erosion or deposition. What link can you see between the line of fastest flow and erosion, and between deposition and areas of still or slow-moving water?

Meander bends are also good places to investigate variations in the depth of the water in the stream, in the way described on pages 10-11. When you have made all these observations, you should be in a position to write an account of your field-work entitled "The Features of Stream Meanders".

After you have studied the physical features of the meandering stream, see if you can find any evidence that people have tried to control the stream processes – perhaps a farmer has tried to strengthen some parts of the banks. If there is any evidence of this kind, try to work out why it was necessary to interfere with the stream.

Over long periods of time the shape of meanders changes considerably as they move across a flood plain. Evidence of these changes can be seen in the formation of "oxbow lakes", sometimes called "meander cut-offs". See what you can find out about oxbow lakes from the reference books in your library.

~~~~~Rapids and Waterfalls~~~~~

One of the most exciting forms of water sport is white-water canoeing – a spectacular event in which competing canoeists have to guide their flimsy craft down a series of waterfalls and rapids, pitting their strength and skills against the force of the current. Rapids and waterfalls are caused by unevenness in the gradient of a stream as it descends from the source to the mouth. Eventually, after millions of years, if nothing were to happen to interrupt the process of erosion (like an earthquake, for example), the gradient of a stream would be worn down to a smooth curve. Waterfalls and rapids are an indication of how much more erosion is possible.

You can find rapids and waterfalls anywhere along the course of a stream, though they are found more often in the upper reaches than in the lower reaches because the steepest descent is usually nearer the source. The diagram shows how Sour Milk Ghyll, a stream in the Lake District, descends from its source in Easedale Tarn to its mouth in Grasmere Lake. From the diagram you can see that the stream falls over 200 metres in all, but most of this is accounted for in the first two kilometres where there are many rapids and waterfalls. In the remaining three kilometres the stream's course is much more even.

This kind of diagram, which is rather like a graph, shows the shape of the "long profile" of the stream. The distance from Easedale Tarn to Grasmere Lake is only 3 kilometres as the crow flies, but in the diagram all the bends in Sour Milk Ghyll have been included and straightened out to show the full length of the stream, which is about 4 kilometres. With the help of your teacher you can draw a diagram to show the long profile of any stream, provided that you have a map showing the changes in height along its course. Our diagram was drawn from the OS 1:50,000 map. From your diagram you can easily see which sections of the stream have the steepest gradients and where rapids and waterfalls are most likely to be found.

If you have the opportunity to study a waterfall or rapid, even a small one, you may be able to work out why it is there (i.e. what has caused the uneven gradient). Sometimes the reason is simply that the land over which the stream flows is steep and irregular – like a mountain side. In other places it may be that the rocks on the downstream side are softer than those upstream, and because they have eroded more quickly, a sharp fall has resulted – as in the photograph. Try to estimate how far the water falls. Does it fall in a single drop, or are there several steps which make a cascade? If your waterfall is large enough, you may find that the water tumbles into a wide, deep pool called a "plunge-pool". How do you think this could have been formed?

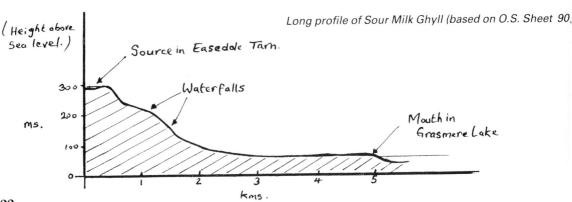

Long profile of Sour Milk Ghyll (based on O.S. Sheet 90.

There are at least four stages in this waterfall and the overall height is about 15 metres. Notice the width and relatively still water of the plunge-pool.

Valleys

~~~~~~

Every stream has a valley. The erosion work of the stream is concentrated within the channel and as the years become decades and then centuries the stream slowly deepens and widens the path along which it flows. At the same time, other erosion processes like weathering are acting on the land, too. In this way, the present shape of the valley has been formed although, of course, it has taken millions of years and it will keep on changing. Since long before modern man inhabited the earth, the streams have been carving their valleys into the land. The mountains and hills between the valleys are simply those bits of the land surface which have been less eroded. In time, even these higher areas will also be removed. Valleys are therefore stages in the general wearing-away and lowering of the land surface.

Although all valleys have similar origins and development, the detailed shape of each valley is unique. Some valleys are deep and narrow with steep sides leading directly away from the banks of the stream. Other streams have valleys which are much wider. Instead of steep slopes close to the banks, there may be low, flat areas next to the channel, as in the photograph. These areas of flat ground beside a stream are known as "flood plains", because they are normally covered with water when the stream overflows its banks after very heavy rain.

Flood plains vary in width, but if you follow a line away from the stream directly across the flood plain you eventually reach a point where

The line of trees clearly marks the course of the stream and the flat areas of the flood plain are evident on both sides of the channel. Through the trees you can just see the break of slope which marks the outer edge of the flood plain. What do you notice about the location of the houses in the photograph?

the ground begins to rise more sharply. This "break of slope" marks the outer edge of the flood plain and the beginning of the valley-side slope. The break of slope between the flood plain and the valley side can be seen in several of the photographs in this book. The map extract here shows part of the valley of the River Stour in Kent. You can see where the flood plain ends and the valley-side slope begins by studying the contour lines. Where there are no contours, or where the contours are widely spaced, the land is probably fairly level; that's the flood plain. The valley side is indicated where the contours are closer together – and the closer the contours, the steeper the slope.

It is usually quite easy to describe not only the slopes but also the shape and size of valleys from the contour patterns on maps, particularly the OS maps at scales of 1:25,000 and 1:50,000. If you want to find out more about contours you will be able to find books in your library which help to explain them. (Some are listed at the end of this book.)

If you have a suitable map, choose one river valley and copy (or trace) the line of the stream and the shapes of the contours. See if you can distinguish a flood plain and a valley side, and shade them in different ways. Use the scale on the map to measure the width of the valley and find out how deep it is by comparing the contour heights. Make a list of all the other information the map gives you about the valley and write an account of how the valley is used by people. When you next visit a stream, try to decide which of the following descriptions fits it best:

(i)   narrow valley with steep sides;
(ii) wide valley with gently sloping sides;
(iii) something in between.

If there is a flood plain, does it stretch

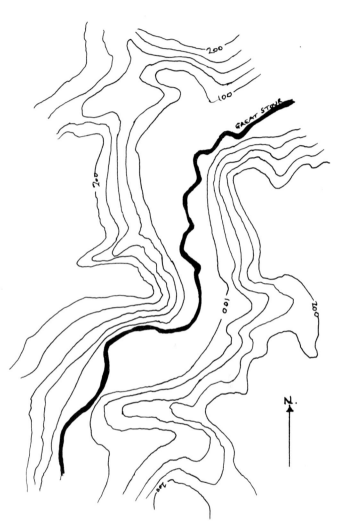

Between Ashford and Canterbury the valley of the River Stour has a well-developed flood plain. The edge of the flood plain is indicated by the 100-foot contour. (Based on O.S. Sheet TRO5, 1:25,000.)

continuously on each side of the stream, or is it on one side only, or in patches only? Walk from the stream up the valley side and make some notes on the uses which people make of the land, paying special attention to any flood plain areas.

Stream Networks

It is important to remember that any small stream which you may choose to study and measure will not continue as a separate channel all the way to the sea. It belongs to a family of streams and rivers which are linked together because they flow into each other. If you follow your stream downwards you will find it is eventually joined by other streams which flow in from one side or the other. Wherever two streams flow together the smaller one is known as the "tributary". Your stream might be the tributary of an important river like the River Thames or the River Trent — or it might even be the main source (the "headwaters" we say) of such a river. You can find out to which river system your stream belongs by following its course on the OS 1:50,000 map.

This linked system of streams and tributaries forms what is called a river "network". Such a network is illustrated in the first diagram. This particular example is part of the network of the River Wear, which flows eastward from the Pennines and enters the North Sea near Sunderland. A map of a complete river network shows you the area of land which is drained by that particular network. This area is called a "drainage basin". Our diagram was drawn by tracing all the blue drainage lines from part of the OS 1:50,000, sheet 87. You can draw a similar map of the stream network in your area from your own local sheet of the OS 1:50,000 map. Compare your drainage

The drainage network of the headwaters of the River Wear (based on O.S. Sheet 87, 1:50,000).

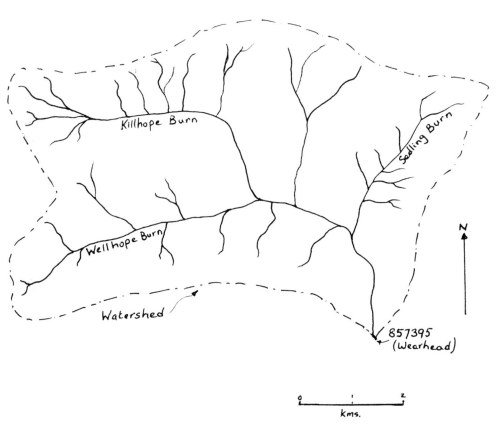

network with our example and see if you can find any similarities between the two patterns.

Like a fingerprint, the pattern of each stream network is unique; you will not find exactly the same pattern anywhere else in the world. Nevertheless, all networks do have some common characteristics. These common features provide those people who study rivers (hydrologists) with an interesting method of measuring and comparing streams which you can try out on your local network.

This method is quite different from the kind of stream measurements described in this book so far (width, depth, and so on). It is called "stream ordering" and is illustrated in the second diagram. The number "1" is given to every small stream where drainage first appears on a map. These are called "first-order" streams. Where two first-order streams join together, they form a "second-order" stream, which is given the number "2". Two second-order streams combine to form a "third-order" stream, given the number "3", and so on. Follow the diagram carefully, and then see if you can "order" the streams in the network you have drawn of your local area. You can use this method to make comparisons of stream networks by counting the number of streams of different orders.

A third-order network and drainage basin.

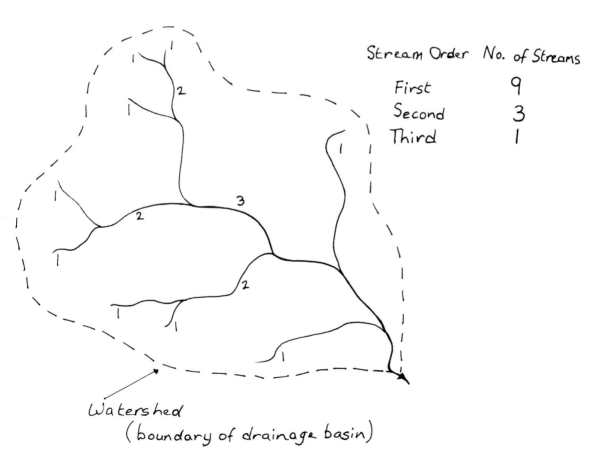

Stream Order	No. of Streams
First	9
Second	3
Third	1

Watershed
(boundary of drainage basin)

~~~~~Underground Streams ~~~~

On pages 16-17 you saw how the energy in the flow and load of a stream works to erode the channel. There is another kind of erosion – chemical erosion – which can produce spectacular features in certain rocks. The rain and snow which are the source of water for all streams contain small quantities of acid. This acid is formed when carbon dioxide gas in the atmosphere is absorbed by droplets of water. The acid is usually very weak but it is strong enough to dissolve certain kinds of rocks, especially chalk and limestone. Nowadays, because of the pollution of the atmosphere by waste gases, rainfall is becoming much more acidic, and "acid rain" is itself causing the pollution of lakes and rivers.

If you know of any old buildings which are made of limestone (e.g. an old church), you can often see the effect of chemical erosion on carvings in the stonework. Carvings which have been sheltered from the weather remain sharp and clear, whereas those which have been exposed to the wind and the rain may have become severely corroded.

The rain which falls in limestone areas sinks into the ground through cracks in the rocks. The acid which is present in the rain gets to work dissolving those parts of the limestone next to the cracks, which gradually become wider. One particular kind of limestone, called Carboniferous Limestone, contains large numbers of these cracks (or "joints" as they are sometimes called), some of them vertical and some horizontal. Because of this it is very common in Carboniferous Limestone areas for streams to "disappear" underground into a whole series of inter-connected holes in the rock, and then re-appear at the surface further down the valley (see the diagram).

When streams in limestone areas disappear from the surface, the valleys in which they used to flow are called "dry valleys". These features are common in limestone areas and you can find out where they occur in Britain, by consulting a geology map in a good atlas. Find the colour for Carboniferous Limestone in the key and then make a list of the areas, noting the names of any hills and nearby towns (e.g. the Mendip Hills, near Cheddar). If you study an OS map (1:50,000 or 1:25,000) of these limestone areas, you will find many examples of dry valleys where the stream in the bottom suddenly stops and then begins again further down the valley.

Typical stream drainage in a limestone area (e.g. the River Axe in the Mendips).

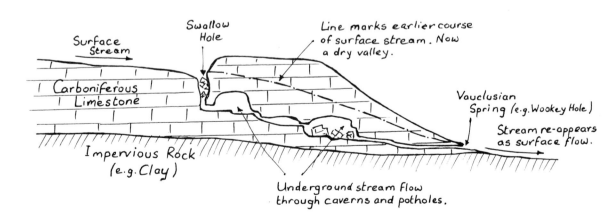

~~~~~~~~~~~~~~~~~~~~~~~~~~~~~~~~

Every stream has a valley but not every valley has a stream. Why is this? The absence of the stream in this dry valley is emphasized by the sinuous line of the dry-stone wall.

The holes down which streams in limestone areas disappear are called "swallow holes" or "pot holes". Pot-holing (or caving) is a popular recreation in these areas, though it can be dangerous and is best done by joining a club which has experts. Some of the most famous underground caves can be visited by the public. There is a list of them here. If you look them up in an encyclopaedia you can find out more about the work of the underground streams.

Underground Streams and Caves in England and Wales

Dan-yr-ogof Caves; Craig-y-nos, Brecon
Ingleborough Cave; near Clapham,
   W. Yorkshire
White Scar Caves; near Ingleton,
   W. Yorkshire
Wookey Hole; near Cheddar, Somerset
Cox's Cavern; near Cheddar, Somerset
Poole's Cavern; near Buxton,
   Derbyshire

These are a few of the natural caves found in areas of limestone scenery which are open to the public.

Streams and Boundaries ~~~

For thousands of years people all over the world have found it convenient to use streams of all sizes to indicate the limits of the ownership of land. At the smallest scale, this might mean a tiny brook forming the boundary between two parishes. For example, in Lincolnshire, the Waithe Beck forms part of the boundary between Brigsley and Ashby-cum-Fenby. At the other end of the scale, the River Danube forms part of the international boundaries of seven European countries.

It is easy to see why streams are so popular as boundaries. Of all natural features they provide the clearest line – much more definite than a line of hills, for example. Moreover, they can easily be shown on a map by drawing a wiggly line!

In this area of Lincolnshire the Waithe Beck is used to mark part of the parish boundaries of seven parishes.

In Britain, most of our major rivers were used in the past to mark the boundaries of the old counties or "shires", as they were sometimes called. In southern England the course of the River Thames down to London provided a succession of boundaries for Gloucestershire, Wiltshire, Oxfordshire, Berkshire, Buckinghamshire, Surrey and Middlesex. The old historic boundaries were considerably altered in 1974, but some sections of the Thames boundaries have survived right up to the present time. See if you can find them in your atlas.

Find out how many of your local parish and district boundaries are streams and rivers. You can do this by examining an OS map on a scale of 1:50,000 (even better, 1:25,000). Look for the various symbols which are used to indicate the different kinds of boundary shown (national, county, district, parish) and copy them out so that you remember them. Make a tracing of

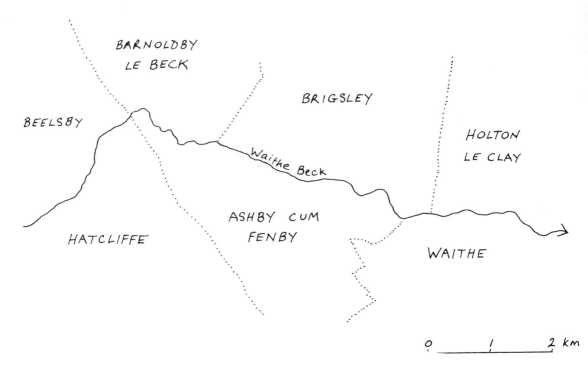

your local area, including all the boundaries you can find, together with all the local streams. Add the main place names and stream names. Now you are in a position to write a short account entitled "Boundaries and Streams in the Local Area".

Using a general atlas map of Britain, see how many rivers you can find which are used, even for a short distance, as county boundaries. Then look at a map of Europe and see how many countries you can find where the international boundary is formed by a river.

Although streams are extremely convenient features to use as boundaries, there are

In the past the River Tyne formed the boundary between Northumberland and Durham. Nowadays Newcastle (on the right of the photograph) and Gateshead (on the left) both lie within the new county of Tyne and Wear.

occasions when problems can arise. Where, for example, would you place a boundary in a river which is, say, ten metres wide? Can you think of alternative positions which might cause arguments? Again, if a boundary is supposed to be fixed for ever, can you think of any problem which might develop over a long period of time, as a result of erosion?

Bridges and Fords

Have you ever found it necessary, during a walk in the countryside, to search for a suitable place to cross a stream? What kind of place do you look for? Somewhere where the channel is narrow enough to jump, perhaps, or where boulders can be used as stepping stones? When bridges are built, the place chosen often depends on local variations in the nature of the stream: for example, the width of the channel, the height and strength of the banks, the danger of flooding.

Finding a suitable place to cross a stream is a problem which people have had to solve from the earliest times, and many important towns in Britain first grew at "bridging points". London itself grew up around the place chosen by the Romans as their main crossing point of the River Thames. The lowest crossing point on a river (i.e. the place with the last bridge before the sea) often became an important port. Why do you think this happened? On this page there is a list of towns which have at some time been important lowest bridging points.

Towns which have been lowest bridging points

King's Lynn
Ipswich
Gloucester
Chepstow
Exeter
Chester
Preston
Stockton
Gainsborough
Selby
Stirling
Perth

Find out from your atlas on which rivers they stand.

Bridges are important because they shorten the travelling distance between places where a stream would otherwise make a detour necessary. Before the Severn Bridge was built, a journey from Bristol to Newport would have taken you through Gloucester. Use your atlas to find out how much distance has been saved by going across the Severn Bridge. You can find out about bridges in your area by studying an Ordnance Survey map (scale 1:50,000). Decide which is your largest local river and draw a sketch map to show the position of all the bridges (road, rail and foot-bridges). Imagine you have been given the job of planning a new bridge in your area, and discuss with your friends the advantages and disadvantages of various sites. Mark your new bridge on your sketch map.

Small streams are usually fairly easy to bridge – sometimes with just a tree trunk, perhaps. Where streams have shallow sections they can be crossed by a ford. We still have a good many fords in Britain, usually in rural areas, and fords are very common in much of the Third World. Before the era of modern technology the only way of bridging a wide stream was to build a series of stone arches, but during the last 200 years the use of iron and steel has made possible the use of different designs. The Severn Bridge is a suspension bridge. Look up "bridges" in an encyclopaedia and see how many different designs you can find.

When engineers build a new bridge they have to take into account not only the best location from the point of view of improving the ease of travel, but also the safest place. Look back briefly through pages 10-25 and make a list of all the processes and work of streams which you think might affect the strength and stability of a bridge.

The crossing of the small stream presented few problems for local people. The building of the Severn Bridge (a suspension bridge) linking Southern England and South Wales required modern technology and cost millions of pounds.

Water Mills

Long before electrical power was available at the flick of a switch and before the invention of steam engines, people had to rely upon sources of power that were available naturally in the world around them. These had to be easy to harness, yet sufficiently powerful and constant to be useful. Wind and water were the obvious sources and, in our well-watered land, it was water which came to be the most widely used. Any stream which had a reliable flow of water and a manageable size could be an important resource for a local community.

Well into the nineteenth century streams, therefore, provided important sites for local industries. The milling of farmers' grain, the crushing of mined rock to obtain metal ore or the driving of bellows and hammers to forge and shape iron were the kind of jobs that were powered by water. Water mills harnessed the power in flowing water to drive water wheels like those shown in the photograph. Sometimes, in order to increase the power and ensure a steady flow of water, particularly in dry summers when streams could be in danger of drying up, mill ponds were constructed to store the water. Small channels (sometimes called "leats") were dug to divert water away from the stream into the mill-pond, and the flow of water onto the blades of the water-wheel could then be controlled by sluices.

With the increasing use of coal-fired steam engines in the early nineteenth century, water mills gradually declined in importance and industries moved away from the banks of streams in rural areas into the towns and cities on the coalfields. Water mills fell into disuse

The two water wheels are part of Rossett Mill near Chester and make use of the water power of the River Alun. Are these undershot or overshot wheels?

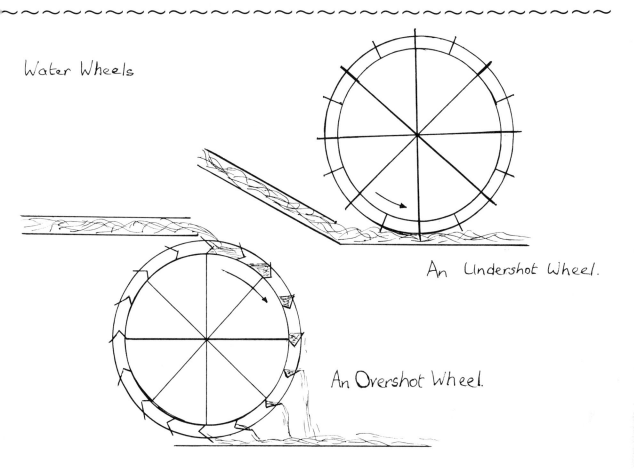

Water Wheels

An Undershot Wheel.

An Overshot Wheel.

and disrepair; weeds and silt began to choke the mill ponds and the idle water wheels gradually rotted away. Many mill buildings have disappeared entirely, but if you are a good detective, there are sometimes clues left in the landscape to show where they used to be – perhaps the name "Mill Street" or an overgrown pond. Old maps of your area can be very useful in this search and you can find these in your local library.

Fortunately, a good many former mill buildings have survived to the present time. Some of them have been taken over and restored to working order by preservation societies interested in local history or industrial archaeology. Most of these restored mills are run as museums and, again, your local library may be able to help you find a working mill that you can visit. Find out when the mill was built and what it was used for. What building materials were used? Was it an overshot or undershot wheel? How was the water collected and directed towards the water wheel? Draw a map to show how the water from the stream was diverted towards the water wheel.

Although these small streams are no longer used as power sources, water itself is still important and the descendants of the small water mills of the past are today's giant hydro-electric power stations, like those built in the mountains of Wales and Scotland. What makes these areas ideal for producing hydro-electric power? Can you think of any advantages in making electricity from water power, rather than from coal or nuclear power?

Flood Control

~~~~~~~~~~ Flood Control ~~~~~~~~~

For most of the time in Britain there is a balance between rainfall and stream discharge; the water that falls upon the surfaces collects in stream channels and drains away through the river network. But once in a while that balance gets disturbed by an exceptionally heavy rainstorm and the sudden increase in water is more than the stream channel can contain. No matter how much faster the stream flows, the water level continues to rise and eventually overflows on to the surrounding fields, across roads and into homes. We say the stream has "burst its banks".

Flooding occurs mainly in the winter months when we receive most of our rainfall and when the ground is often waterlogged. The damage caused by flood waters is not simply that of making things sodden, smelly and musty. The rapid increase in the volume and speed of flood waters creates a lot of extra energy (see pages 8-9) and that energy can be a destructive force, sweeping away bridges and buildings and drowning any farm animals unable to reach the safety of high ground. River floods, together with tornadoes, earthquakes and volcanoes, are natural hazards of the environment which societies throughout history have had to face. Make a list of the natural hazards that you can recall as memorable events of history; the Bible will provide you with a number of examples.

Because of the enormous damage which can be caused by floods, people from the earliest times have tried to reduce the danger. In places where the flood risks are recognized as very great (e.g. flood plain areas), people have simply avoided building on the land and it is left as meadowland or open space. Many recreation parks in London, for example, can be found on the flood plains alongside the tributary streams of the River Thames – for instance, Hyde Park. Where there is a flood danger in a built-up area, it has been necessary in some cases to alter the stream so that the storm waters can flow away more quickly. The photograph shows a stream which has been made more "efficient" – its course has been straightened and a deep concrete culvert now directs the water quickly and smoothly downstream. Sometimes the culvert is

covered over and the stream is converted into an underground storm drain.

Find out if there are any neighbourhoods where you live which sometimes suffer from flooding. The places most at risk are the low-lying areas, so you can draw a map to show where these are. An OS 1:50,000 map will help you, because it shows the variation in the height of the land. Work out where the lowest areas are and shade them in. Then you can find out from your local council whether they have had to take any special measures (like the construction of culverts) to prevent flooding. After periods of heavy rain, keep an eye on your local paper for flood reports and find out where they are from.

This is the River Ravensbourne in south London. The concrete culvert provides a more effective channel than a natural stream for coping with storm water which used to cause flooding. Why do you think this culvert is more effective?

Lost Streams

The maps show an area of south London as it was in 1898 and then as it was in 1936. There are many more roads and houses on the later map and the difference between the two maps provides a clear indication of the enormous growth in population which took place in the London suburbs. The difference, though, is not just the new buildings; also, some of the features of the original landscape have disappeared from the map.

Look carefully and you will see that in 1898 there was a stream flowing from the bend of the road in the south west corner along a little valley. On the 1936 map, however, this stream is no longer shown. The stream itself is still there, of course, but its channel now consists of an underground pipe fed by storm-water drains along the road-side and in the gardens of the houses.

Sometimes the course of a former stream is indicated in the name of a road or street. In London, for example, three small streams which were surface features in Roman and medieval times – the Holbourne, the Walbrook and the Fleet – have all given their names to roads. The streams themselves are still there, down beneath the concrete, still carrying the rain which falls on the City of London away into the River Thames.

When new buildings are planned, the engineers have to take great care to make sure that any development which takes place does not interfere with the natural drainage of the land. All streams, even those which only flow occasionally, after heavy rain, have to be accurately located and linked by pipes to the natural stream network. In effect, these pipes become a man-made section of the network.

The arrow between fields numbered 55 and 65 shows that a stream was flowing in this part of Bromley in 1898. By 1936 new houses had been built and the stream had disappeared. Are there any features of the 1898 map (below) which survive on the 1936 map (right below)?

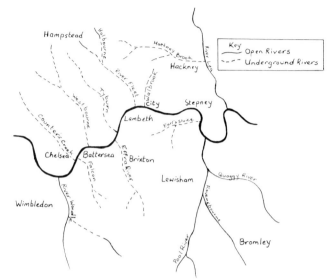

This work has to be done very carefully, with the correct gradients and size of pipes; otherwise, flooding may occur after heavy rainfall. If there are any streets in your neighbourhood which sometimes suffer from flooding, this may be an indication that there used to be a stream there. Perhaps street names will provide a clue too.

You can find out about the lost streams in your area in two ways. First, you can visit your public library and ask to see the old maps. The most useful are the old Ordnance Survey 25-inch plans. You have to look hard to find the streams because they are shown in black, like all the other details. When you have found them, ask the librarian if you may make a tracing of the streams. (They may prefer to make you a photocopy, and you can make your tracing from that.) Compare this with the modern 25-inch (1:2,500) plan and see how many of your streams are still marked.

The other source of information is the

The lost rivers of London.

engineer's department of your local council, where you should be able to obtain or consult a map of the storm-water drains in your area. If you compare this map with your tracing you can find out if any of the streams have been converted into underground drains.

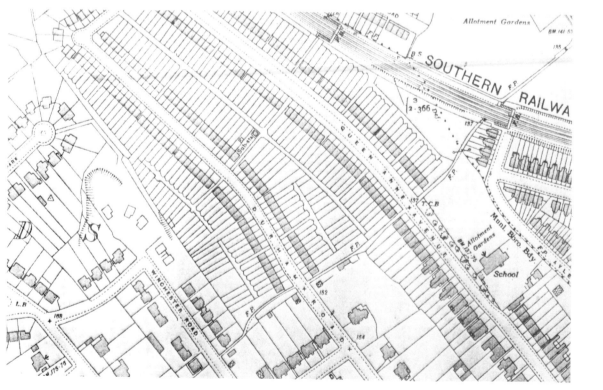

~~~~Recreation and Pastimes~~~

There is something especially attractive about the sight and sound of running water. People of all ages find relaxation and enjoyment in pottering around a stream – or just sitting and listening, and watching the never-ending movement of the water. In the eighteenth century the fortunate owners of great private estates like Blenheim and Chatsworth were very aware of the importance of water and they employed skilful landscape designers to create a pleasing variety of streams, lakes and waterfalls. Later, in the nineteenth century, the public parks of our industrial towns, where ordinary people could walk in the evenings and at week-ends, were often planned around streams or beside rivers. Nowadays, rivers and streams provide literally millions of people with opportunities for organized and casual recreation.

Almost every part of Britain has its favourite local stream or river where you can be certain to find crowds of people during a fine week-end in summer. Sometimes there is a special natural feature which provides the main attraction – a waterfall, a pool where children can paddle, a small area of flood plain for playing games or having picnics, or a little beach on the inside bend of a meander.

Sadly, there are times when the pleasure ends in tragedy, because the stream processes described in this book can prove dangerous – usually in places where the water is deep and currents are strong, and especially under flood conditions when the power of the water can sweep away the strongest swimmer.

The most popular places for recreation are sometimes called "honey-pots" (why do you think we use this phrase?) and their popularity often brings problems. The constant wearing of the land by countless thousands of pairs of

Angling is the most popular outdoor recreation in Britain.

Do not be misled by the calm appearance of this river. Beneath the surface there are powerful currents.

The members of this canoe-club are practising their skills on the River Medway at Yalding.

feet each year can kill the vegetation and erode the banks. Also, because many people are thoughtless, the accumulation of rubbish causes pollution.

Not all kinds of recreational activity can go on happily side-by-side – we say they are not always "compatible". Look at the activities in two of the photographs here. In what ways could they spoil each other? Make a list of all the stream-based recreational activities you can think of, and then divide them into groups of compatible activities. What kind of stream conditions are ideal for each of the pastimes you have listed? What kind of stream features do you think different age-groups look for, for their leisure and recreation?

Find out from your local council (probably the parks department) how much use they make of streams in the parks and recreational areas in your neighbourhood. Visit these places and see for yourself whether the streams are being used successfully. Is there anything you think the council could do to improve these amenities?

Pollution

The pollution of the environment is a serious problem in many parts of the world, not least in some parts of Britain. Pollution occurs when so much waste accumulates that it causes damage to the environment and its natural life forms. Pollution also causes unpleasantness for people, and can be dangerous to health. Streams are particularly vulnerable to pollution because, from time immemorial, people have used the natural drainage network as a cheap and convenient way of getting rid of waste materials. In the distant past, most of these wastes consisted of sewage, but as our society became more industrialized and technically advanced, industrial wastes too were tipped into rivers.

Up to a point, a stream can cope with most kinds of waste products, because the micro-organisms in the water act on the wastes and gradually clean things up. Pollution occurs

~~~~~~

when so much waste enters the stream that this natural cleaning system becomes overloaded. When that happens, the more advanced forms of water life, such as beetles and fish, can no longer live in the water. In a very real sense, therefore, the stream "dies".

Pollution is not always caused deliberately. Sometimes it is accidental. One example is the pollution of streams in the countryside by fertilizers which are washed out of the fields by rain. This fertilizer makes the water so rich that it encourages the excessive growth of water plants which cover the water surface like a green carpet, especially in summer. Find out if there are any streams in your area affected like this.

For many years now we have been aware of the problem of pollution, and in Britain the government has passed laws which control the kinds of material which can be poured into the rivers and streams. You can find out how sewage and other wastes are dealt with in your area by writing to your local council or to the regional office of the Department of the Environment. You might even be able to visit a sewage works.

The study of water pollution is a very scientific subject, and it is difficult to find out about it without using technical equipment. If you want to go deeply into this subject, you will have to ask your local librarian for specialized books.

There is one aspect of stream pollution which you can study without specialized scientific knowledge, and this is the problem illustrated in the photograph. The pollution of streams by rubbish is a particular problem with streams which run near or through towns and cities. Why do you think this is so? What do you think the authorities can do to improve the situation? Make a survey of the streams in your local area to find out if there are any places where pollution by rubbish is a problem, and try to work out why it happens at these particular spots.

◁ Rubbish in streams is unsightly and can be dangerous. Why do you think some people get rid of their rubbish in this way?

~~~Planning and Management~~

Because there are several different ways in which we might want to use the resources of a stream and its valley, it is sometimes difficult to decide which kind of use should have priority. As we saw on pages 40-41, not all kinds of activity can go happily side-by-side, and we have to be careful that one use of a stream does not automatically spoil things for other uses. A typical example of this kind of problem is found in the valley of the Great Stour in Kent. In this valley there are valuable farm lands and gravel beds, together with attractive recreational areas and important wildlife habitats. What conflicts of interest do you think could arise between (i) farmers, (ii) gravel extractors, (iii) water sportsmen and (iv) naturalists?

The responsibility for making sure that the local people get the benefits of all the resources of the Great Stour valley rests with the Kent County Council and the four district councils in the area. They hope that they have found the answer to this difficult problem by drawing up the Stour Valley Countryside Plan. This plan was published in 1982, after a great amount of detailed survey work to find out as much as possible about the resources of the valley and the activities of all the various interest groups. What the plan does is to suggest which activities should have priority in different parts of the valley, in a way which the council hopes that local people will think is fair.

You can see on the right a small part of the Stour Valley Countryside Plan for a stretch of the valley near Canterbury. Just north of the village of Stodmarsh is a large area of open water and marshland which has been a National Nature Reserve since 1968 because of its outstanding importance to bird-life. Part of this reserve consists of old gravel workings. The river is also used by motor cruisers, dinghies and rowing boats, for which there are moorings. Although most of the area is farmland, some of the landscapes are considered to be especially attractive. Note also that there is an area where sand and gravel working will be allowed, and one where the tipping of waste is permitted.

There is nothing unusual about the problems of managing the Stour valley. Similar problems of conflicting demands can

The cover of the Stour Valley Countryside Plan illustrates five demands made on the resources of the river. Can you say what they are?

Kent County Council   March 1982

Stour Valley Countryside Plan

Written Statement

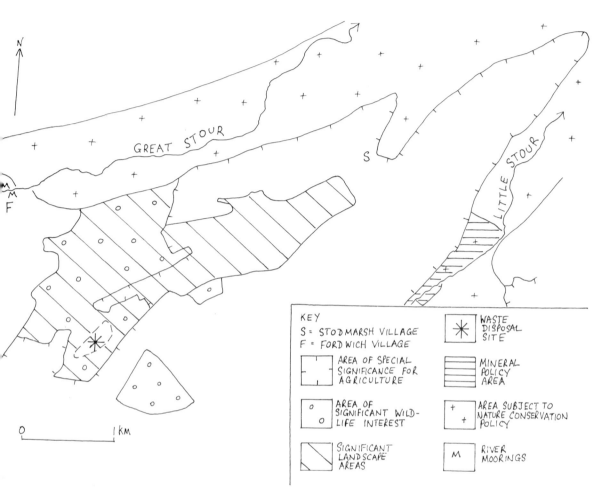

KEY
S = STODMARSH VILLAGE
F = FORDWICH VILLAGE

□ AREA OF SPECIAL SIGNIFICANCE FOR AGRICULTURE

○ AREA OF SIGNIFICANT WILD-LIFE INTEREST

⬚ SIGNIFICANT LANDSCAPE AREAS

✳ WASTE DISPOSAL SITE

▤ MINERAL POLICY AREA

+ AREA SUBJECT TO NATURE CONSERVATION POLICY

M RIVER MOORINGS

be found in most valleys. Find out from your local authority whether any studies have been made of streams in your area, and whether any management plans have been drawn up. If no such scheme exists, you could make your own survey of a small area and produce a map similar to the one here.

This map is based upon one of the maps in the Stour Valley Countryside Plan. It shows how Kent County Council and the local district councils hope to avoid conflict between different uses of the river valley.

Difficult Words

~~~~~~~~   ~~~~~~~~

attrition	This is the word for the way materials such as pebbles, boulders, etc, in the stream channel are gradually broken and worn down into smaller, more rounded fragments by being knocked against each other in the force of flowing water.
bank-full	A stream is bank-full when the stream channel is full, with the flowing water level with the top of the river banks. If the water level rises any more, the water would then flow over the banks and spill on to the flood plain alongside the stream channel.
break of slope	The point at which there is a noticeable change in the steepness or gradient of a slope.
bridging point	A point or place at which a river is, or could be, bridged. (The lowest bridging point generally marks the upstream limit of ocean navigation.)
channel	The channel is the narrow trough which is shaped by the force of flowing water. It consists of the river or stream bed and the banks on either side.
chemical erosion	The wearing away of rocks by chemical processes such as solution and oxidation. Chemical erosion is sometimes known as *corrosion* and causes the rocks to disintegrate and change in appearance.
current	The distinct and defined movement of water in the stream channel.
delta	An area and feature of deposition formed where a stream or river flows into a sea or lake. The term was first used by the Greeks who noticed the resemblance between the delta of the River Nile and their own letter △ (delta).
deposition	The laying down of material which has been transported or carried by running water. Material deposited by running water is known as alluvium. Deltas are depositional features consisting of alluvium.
downstream	The direction in which the water is flowing.
drainage basin	The total area of land drained by a stream or a single river network. The boundary line of the drainage basin is the watershed. All the rain that falls inside the boundary of the watershed will drain into that stream or river network.
energy	The energy created by running water is the power to do "work". The energy of the stream is used to erode the bed and banks of the channel, to transport sediment and to maintain the flow of water. When you stand in a stream you can feel the energy of the water as it flows past your legs.
erosion	The wearing-away and removal of rock by running water, ice, wind and waves. These are known as the agents of erosion.
flood plain	The floor of a valley over which a river may spread in time of flood, depositing alluvium. It is an area of almost flat land which borders the stream or river channel.
ford	The shallow part of a river which can be easily crossed. A common place name for a riverside settlement: e.g. Washford, Arlesford, Oxford, etc.
gradient	The steepness of a surface or slope, like a hillside or river bed.
gravel	Water-worn stones which are usually rounded by attrition and range in diameter size from 2 mm to 60 mm.
honey-pot	A term used to describe a popular place which attracts visitors and tourists. Stonehenge is one such place. Honey-pots can easily become overcrowded.
hydro-electricity	The making of electricity by using water power to turn the turbines which are modern water-wheels.
hydrology	The scientific study of water, especially the water which falls and flows on the land.
industrial arch-aeology	The study and preservation of old industrial machines and processes. At places like Ironbridge, Blaenavon and Stoke-on-Trent old factories and mines and their machines have been restored to working order so that we can understand how things used to be made as well as how people used to earn their living.
load	The amount of material such as pebbles, sediment, alluvium, etc, which is transported within and by a stream or river. The load will vary according to the velocity and volume of water flowing in the channel. The greater the velocity and volume the more energy is created to carry a bigger load.
long profile	The long profile of a stream is the variation in gradient along the length of the river bed from source to mouth.
meander	A curved, loop-like bend in the course of a stream or river. A meandering stream invariably has a well-developed flood plain.

natural hazards	The dangers and disasters caused by extremes of wind and weather (e.g. hurricanes and hailstorms), flooding, tidal waves, earthquakes, etc. We cannot control the destructive energy created by natural hazards but a great deal of research is being done to help predict when and where such events are likely to occur.
network	A number of drainage channels, from tributary streams to the main drainage channel, which link together to convey all the surface flow of water within a drainage basin to the one main channel and exit point.
oxbow lake	Part of a meander which has been cut off from the river channel as the river has slowly changed its course. The meander section becomes separated from the main channel and is left as a small horse-shoe-shaped lake in the river's flood plain.
pebble	A small, water-rounded stone larger than gravel but smaller than a cobble. A pebble is worn and shaped largely by attrition and the action of flowing water. A pebble is defined by size and ranges in diameter between 60 mm and 64 mm (see table on page 12).
sediment	Materials such as clay particles, grains of silt, sand and pieces of rock which are laid down by water. The smallest particles are carried by streams and rivers from the land and deposited as layers of sediment on the ocean floor. These sediments in millions of years will form new sedimentary rocks.
sewage	Human and animal waste.
silt	Small particles of sediment laid down in water. Alluvium is composed mainly of silt-sized particles which range in diameter from 0.002 mm to 0.02 mm (see table on page 12). Silt particles are larger than clay but smaller than sand.
sinuous	Winding. A meandering river has a sinuous channel.
suspension bridge	A bridge built so that the section of the roadway across the water is hung or suspended from steel cables. The cables are stretched across the water from towers on each side of the river.
tributary	A stream or river which joins a larger one.
upstream	The direction along the river opposite to the flow of water; that is, "uphill" against the current.
valley	An elongated depression in the land surface sloping downstream towards the sea or inland lake. Valleys are largely the results of flowing water eroding and removing material along the drainage channel which occupies or used to occupy the floor of the valley.
velocity	The speed of flowing water measured generally in centimetres per second; that is the number of centimetres that a unit of water will travel in one second. The greater the velocity the greater the energy created by flowing water.

~~~~~~~~~~~~ Book List ~~~~~~~~~~~~

Books marked with an asterisk (*) are most suitable for the teacher's use only.

Angel, H., *The World of a Stream,* Faber, 1976

*Bentley, J.C. et al, *The Use of Maps in School,* Basil Blackwell, 1975

Brown, J.H., *Elementary Geographical Fieldwork,* Blackie, 1978

Collins-Longman, *Atlas Three,* Collins-Longman, 1973

Crisp, T., *Rivers,* Nelson, 1979

*Cullingford, C.H.D., *British Caving,* Routledge, Kegan and Paul, 1964

E.P. Ltd., *Map Reading,* Educational Productions Ltd, 1976

Fullagar, A.P. and Virgo, H.E., *Map Reading in Local Studies,* Hodder & Stoughton, 1984

*Knapp, B.J., *Earth and Man,* George Allen and Unwin, 1982

*Lewin, J., *British Rivers,* George Allen and Unwin, 1981

Mason, E.J., *Caves and Caving in Britain,* Robert Hale, 1977

Matkin, R.B., *Maps and Map Reading,* Faber, 1970

*Mills, D., *Geographical Work in Primary and Middle Schools,* Geographical Association, 1981

Schools Council, *Water Pollution: General Studies Project,* Schools Council Publications, 1972

Young, G., *Pollution,* Edward Arnold, 1980

Index